The Honeymoon Voyage

By the same author
Modern Poets 11 (with Peter Redgrove and D.M. Black)
Two Voices
Logan Stone
The Shaft
Love and Other Deaths
Akhmatova: Requiem and Poem without a Hero (translations)

The Honeymoon Voyage

D. M. Thomas

Secker & Warburg · London

First published in England 1978 by
Martin Secker & Warburg Limited
14 Carlisle Street, London W1V 6NN

436 51890 2

To Caitlin and Sean

Printed in Great Britain by
REDWOOD BURN LIMITED
Trowbridge & Esher

Contents

Acknowledgments

Grateful acknowledgments are due to the following in which some of the poems first appeared: *American Scholar*, BBC *(Poetry Now)*, *Critical Quarterly*, *Encounter*, *Little Word Machine*, *London Magazine*, *New Poems 1976–77* (Hutchinson), *New Review, New Statesman, Outposts*, Oxus Press, *Poetry Wales*, Sceptre Press, *Sunday Telegraph Magazine*, *Transatlantic Review, Times Literary Supplement*, and Words Press. **In Her Imagined Person** was commissioned by the Globe Playhouse Trust.

1

The Rock
(from a Japanese creation myth)

I sought you even in Death. Who can ask more?

I am not listening.
I am listening to the whisper of grass
Which I had forgotten.

Am I not more to you than grass?
Talk with me.

You lit the tooth of your comb.
You looked at me, you ran from me,
You threw this rock down between us.
This knowledge is darker than death.

I saw from the spaces that ate your face
That one must become the bird and one the bat.
Where the clockhands stand together, one must stand
In the noon blaze, grieving for the one
Who must stand in the midnight blackness
Where the clockhands stand together, invisible.
Which side am I, in darkness or in light?
Unless you speak the words of separation
My feet cannot move from this spot.

. . . .

Do not weep. Let me not wander
Forever haunted by your pain.

I feel no pain. I am strong,
Stronger than you. It is right
I should be in darkness, you in light.
When our son, Fire, consumed me, being born,
He made me a kiln, I have no feelings.

Surely I shall return, one day, with power
To move the rock.
Who but you can comfort me
For having made you my shadow?

Do not weep, my beloved.
Take up the rock,
And I will enfold you to me.

There is not that in me
Which would move the rock.
If there were,
I should not need your comforting.
The rock cannot be moved.

Diary of a Myth-Boy

Something called Death came today. Witch-
doctor has this big dream,
tells him three canoes sailing down-
stream, Immortal Spirit
in third one. So he lines us all up.
Sure enough, about noon,
canoe comes, full of rotten fruit.
That's Death, says the witch-doctor. White
man comes sailing down in
second canoe, and our stupid
sod of a witch-doctor
wades out and embraces him! Down
comes Immortal Spirit in third
canoe, waving his arms
shouting, That's Death, you fool, can't you
even count up to three?
He just stood, scratching his head and
grinning, he's not all there . . .

Grandmother comes to me in the
night, squats on my face and
farts. If you ask me she's crazy.
This afternoon sharpened
my arrow-heads . . .

                   Followed mother
when she went out gathering
palms to make my penis-sheath. Saw,
as she climbed to the top,
my first cunt, rich as a date. Raped
her. Told grandmother. She
said, You're a big boy now, but watch
out for your father. If he
sends you to the region of souls,
take a hummingbird with
you. Crazier and crazier . . .

Sick all morning. Could this
be pregnancy, or grandmother's
farts? My father in a
terrible temper, tells me to
set out tomorrow for
the region of souls, to fetch a
dance-rattle. Sure thing my
mother's ratted on me, the cow . . .

Grandmother's dead. When she
came last night I stuck an arrow
up her arse. Her guts fell
out. God, she was rotten. No more
entries for a few days.
Lots to write about, I expect,
when I come back . . .

                    Granny
was right about the hummingbird.
Dance-rattle hung from a
cord, hummingbird's beak cut it. It
splashed into the river,
alerted the souls who fired their
arrows in. If I'd been
there I wouldn't be writing this.
Dance-rattle floated to
me. Grandmother wise woman. When
I got home, mother and
sister sick, father away hunting
— I'd like to have seen that
bastard's face. No food cooked . . .

Mother and sister dead, with most
of the other women.
Sister goes to my hut to fetch
dead fish, takes granny's guts
instead. Stupid bitch! It's poison
of course. Everyone who

ate it, died. They call it Disease.
Saves me the bother of
killing mother for tale-telling . . .

No girls left. We boys muck
about among ourselves. We're all
pregnant but can't bear kids.
It's no fun cooking and cleaning,
and with fat bellies too.
What a life! . . .

        Got my revenge on
father today. Put on
antlers, met him out hunting, speared
him. Flung him in the lake.
Spirits must have got him, his lungs
floated up . . .

        Saw this girl,
up a tree, the first for bloody
months. Chatted her up, it
turned out she didn't like fish. I
tried to climb the trunk but
my erection got in the way,
came all over it and
gave up. A crowd of the other
lads came at her through the
treetops, raped her, then cut her up
into little pieces.
Which, as they slid down the trunk, met
my sperm and of course turned
into girls. I got a thick slice
of rump and my girl's well
stacked. Some of them are skin and bone . . .

God it's a boring life,
no tribes to fight with, all killed off
by Disease (grandmother

started something there), my
fat wife a pain in the arse. A
white anthropologist
who's turned up here's been telling me
about life with his folk.
It sounds really exciting. I'm
going to pack a few
pearls and things tonight, slip this
diary under the
anthropologist's tent-flap and
sneak away up river . . .

(Acknowledgments to tribal myths
of Central Brazil)

Ghost

Twin-above-the-dark-Waters woke up one
night to find her bed pitching
                    like a canoe
from her dream. Her father came running.
Daughter, quick, get up!
                    There's an earthquake!

No more peace in the hut. No sooner they
sit down to eat the food she's cooked
                    with flour and with
love, than plates rise and crash into the
roof and the pot smashes.
                    One night her

new hair-tuft's hacked off while she sleeps. Come out
of there, ghost, it's no use you
                    hiding! But the
ghost that slid out of the corner was
not a bit ashamed to be
                    caught out. Ghost,

why are you hurting me? Because I don't
want you to be alive, you
                    stink the hut!
Then, a flood of tears and the ghost tossed
her hair dark as night and
                    withdrew to

hatch more tricks. Twin-above-the-dark-Waters
wasn't sleeping. The eyes that
                    peered out from her
black coils were large and sad. Daughter,
things a bit quieter
                    now, good!

Twin-above-the-dark-Waters wanted to
talk to a true friend, but had
                to make do with
the boy who'd stared at her over his
scythe as though she were plump
                sharp water-

melon. Where you been, filth, first you come in
to my room, blubber, take out your
                mother's wedding-
skirt, then when I wide-awake you off
somewhere! You too much for
                one father.

He beat her so hard she couldn't lie down.
She cried with rage then shouted
                at the corner,
You there, devil, come out of there! The
ghost looked shamefaced when she
                came. Sister,

I didn't mean harm. I've got used to you.
Boy no good for you, though. Why
                no good for me?
you not alive to know, spirit! True,
but I sleep in this hut
                as long as you!

Tomorrow you take me with you, sister.
I'll be no trouble. From what
                you say you need
me to keep an eye on you! For hours
they whispered and the ghost
                licked her lips

and warned her. When she lay in his rough arms
the next time, the ghost whispered
                advice to her

from the long grass. Let him touch you there
a little, sister! And she
                    didn't think

she should but did as the ghost said. Now let
him break your membrane, sister!
                    And she didn't
think it nice but she did as the ghost
said. Now should I close my
                    legs, spirit?

But the ghost had gone away or didn't
seem bothered any more. And
                    in the long moons
that rose and fell, waxed and waned, while she
waited alone in the
                    hut of bad

girls, often she'd say, Won't you come and talk
to me, sister? But the ghost
                    said nothing.

The Dream Game

There was a black girl
who was so beautiful all the white men slept with her.
She had a hunter, an analyst, a manufacturer, and a poet.
And so clever
she picked up their language from their conversations.

She grew unhappy as
she couldn't dream, and not to dream was a kind of
constipation to the black girl, a growing burden
she grew fat with,
so that they had to buy her a pantigirdle.

We'll make you a dream,
said the analyst, and you must guess what it is.
When she had gone he explained to the others, smiling,
they wouldn't make up a dream
for the black girl, she would make up her own.

If her questions, if her guesses,
he said, contain in the last word the letter e, say yes,
if not, say no. The hunter, the manufacturer,
and the poet smiled,
and they called the black girl back into the room.

They instructed her
to ask them each in turn a question about the dream
they had made up for her. She could go on questioning
for as long as
she liked. It was important she find her dream.

How their laughter
exploded at her frequent marvellous guesses.
Black girl, they said, this is black magic! and their
beer spluttered out
of their mouths in uncontrollable mirth as she

unwound her dream, her dream
that all four of them had murdered her with knives,
cut her up in the kitchen and re-cycled her
into trees, into paper
on which beautiful elegies were written about her.

Whale

A whale lay cast up on the island's shore
    in the shallow water of the outgoing tide.
        He struggled to fill his lungs,
        he grew acquainted with weight.

And the people came and said, Kill it, it is food.
And the witch-doctor said, It is sacred, it must not be harmed.
And a girl came and with an empty coconut-shell
    scooped the seawater and let it run over the whale's blue
                bulk.

A small desperate eye showing white all round
    the dark iris. The great head flattened against
        sand as a face pressed against glass.

And a white man came and said, If all the people
    push we can float it off on the next tide.
And the witch-doctor said, It is taboo, it must not be touched.

And the people drifted away.
And the white man cursed and ran off to the next village for
                help.

And the girl stayed.
She stayed as the tide went out.
The whale's breath came in harsh spasms.
Its skin was darkening in the sun.
The girl got children to form a chain
of coconut-shells filled with fresh water
that she poured over his skin.

The whale's eye seemed calmer.

With the high tide the white man came back.
As the whale felt sea reach to his eye he reared

on fins and tail flukes, his spine arced
and he slapped it all down together, a great leap
into the same inert sand.
His eye rolled
in panic as again he lifted and crashed down,
    exhausted, and again lifted and crashed down,
        and again, and again.

The white man couldn't bear his agony and strode away,
    as the tide receded.
He paced and paced the island and cursed God.

Now the whale didn't move.
The girl stroked his head
and as the moon came up
she sang to him
of friends long dead and children grown and gone,
sang like a mother to the whale,

and sang of unrequited love.

And later in the night
    when his breaths had almost lost touch
        she leant her shoulder against his cheek

and told him stories, with many details,
of the mud-skipping fish that lived
    in the mangroves on the lagoon.

Her voice
and its coaxing pauses
was as if fins
were bearing him up to the surface of the ocean
to breathe and see,
as with a clot of blood falling on her brow
the whale passed clear from the body of his death.

(*after an incident in Lyall Watson's* Gifts of Unknown Things)

Ninemaidens
(Stone-circle, West Cornwall)

I

Our sorrow and our joy
Dance with us.
Nine maidens,
We are unaccountable.

Dance with us
The sabbath-dances.
We are unaccountable
For this summer lightning.

The sabbath dances
Astonished,
For this summer lightning
Is love.

Astonished
Our hearts thunder.
Is love
Anything but yes?

Our hearts thunder
With desire for you.
Anything but yes
And we should die.

With desire for you
We are struck dumb.
And we should die
In your arms.

We are struck dumb,
Having too many words.
In your arms
Stone is beautiful.

Having too many words
We close into a circle.
Stone is beautiful.
We open to you.

We close into a circle,
Ninemaidens.
We open to you
Our sorrow and our joy.

II

A stone can sing
The one song.
You ask of me
How long I have waited.

The one song
Has a sad tune.
How long I have waited
For a sign.

Has a sad tune
Frightened you?
For a sign
I will cast spells.

Frightened, you
Do not look at me.
I will cast spells,
Astonishing myself.

Do not look at me
As you enter me,
Astonishing myself,
Stone mixed with rain.

As you enter me
I am
Stone mixed with rain,
I pay the piper.

I am
Love. Whisper to me.
I pay the piper
To vanish.

Love, whisper to me
The true word.
To vanish
Is the only way.

The true word
You ask of me
Is the only way
A stone can sing.

III

We are women
By choice.
Becoming stone
We have lost everything.

By choice
We are naked.
We have lost everything
To give you life.

We are naked
As the newly born.
To give you life
We give you suffering.

As the newly born
You come to us.
We give you suffering
With our milk.

You come to us,
Love us, and go,
With our milk
Fall away.

Love us, and go.
Don't look back.
Fall away.
Stones. Stones.

Don't look back.
We shan't change.
Stones. Stones.
The mouth. The grass.

We shan't change
The way love is,
The mouth the grass
Brings the milk for.

The way love is
Becoming stone
Brings the milk, for
We are women.

2

A Cornish Graveyard at Keweenaw
(N. Michigan)

Harriet Uren, 100, eighty years from Penzance,
Died with the scent of saffron in the cloam.
Daughter and great-grandmother, felt death enter
Like the slow dark voyage down the home coast.
Plymouth was strange, Fowey less; she could not weep
Though grown men wept, as hymn on hymn unrolled
The Lizard, flashing. Then the Mount, the light,
Only a miner's daughter could have seen,
Drawing away as she drew nearer home.

Turned then, bride to groom, and went below.
Undressed in the dense dark, too shy to breathe.
Surrendered to what might come, her eyes chatoyant,
Rocked in fusions
Of gain and loss and that sustaining rise.
Praying only this night what may suffice,
She slept. Couples embrace, weep, talk,
Or sleep. On deck, the Scillies past, the seethe
Of brotherly harmony grows coarse and buoyant.

And here intuited their second life.
That granite outcrop grew them, this grew with them.
Cherished rock more than they cherished flesh, drilled,
Blasted it, as they went, sang as they went.
Stillness in this boomed peninsular
Unrest. Yet so much, and such dry, Cornish
Wit, together! Such eager harmonies
To such handsome voices keen to pitch a tune!
Praise God for the water's lap, the same horn-thrust.

And all in time who went on to unlock
Nevadan silver, Californian gold,
Great pranksters, wrestlers and evangelists,
Wondered before they died or slept
Which was their home, Cornwall or Keweenaw.

The seams of want and wanderlust
Compelled new shafts of love, but those clairvoyant
And helmet eyes still saw a celtic cross
And window-light, their roots their albatross.

Sumach sighs, and the great lake locks in ice.
You are luminescent with impurities,
Tarnished with fractures, silky with inclusions,
Your winks and laughter ride out circumstance,
You prod each other with ironic fists.
Tin into gold, my sonnies, my alchemists,
You who're quicksilver like New Almadén —
Where now? Impossible you'll stay in baulk,
With that swift talk, in pulses, like your sea.

Decks crammed like troopships, or pared, two
By two, hard-rock miners driving into talc,
Ricepaper clinging to honeymoon silk.
I praise God's ship of death, restorative,
Hiding the bone, healing the lung's scar,
And imagine what Liberty has hushed their dry
Expanding stories awhile, their souls raw,
Their eyes bright, moving west across the spectrum
Of hard rock, giving new land new energy.

UNDER CARN BREA

Grandmother

In a room with drawn venetian blinds
I was carried to you, and took from your hands
Green grapes. Though your hands and face frightened
Me, I think, that faded as the grapes brightened.

So much for the dark drawing-room.
So much for death-candles in the gloom.
At eighteen months of my life, grapes glowed
The green of greens, a light, a beatitude.

Mona

Mona turned all language to a comic
Amazement at catastrophe barely averted.
'My *gar,* Harold! What did you *do?*'
Round eyes puckering to chuckles at a new
Panic and wonder, 'My *life,*
HARold!' Left every phrase on the rise
Dazzled in its natural drama.

Nothing happened at the creek
That week each summer. I was puzzled
Why parents didn't need to play, just laugh
In tune with Mona's anguished shrieks
At Harry's bloodies and buggers as he guzzled
The fish he'd caught. The lamp lit,
Harry in bed, Mona did exercises,

Groaned, bumped and thumped, showed how far
Snapped suspenders sank back in the fat.
'I'n it *shameful!*' Whooped her anguish.
'Mona you're obscene.' Kneaded more flesh,
Found more. 'AMy!' chuckled and thumped. 'My *gar!*

Harold, did you *ever*!' I understood,
Half-asleep in my mother's lap,
Everything aquiver, it was good.

Harold

When you laughed, at your own joke or another's,
To the damned and God himself it carried.
Which came back to you, amplifying your laughter.
God shook then over all the wheatfields.
Making you throw your head back and split the ceiling.
God suffered agonies in his own chapels.
Back went your head, blasting the rooftops.
If it rained it was God's helpless tears.

Ben Wearne

'Think of his dear mother, she could 'ardly stan', crawlin'
About on 'er 'ands and knees, I expec' she was,
Beatin' 'er 'ead on the ground, 'cause 'er *dear Son*,
'Er dear *cheel*, was in *hagony*' (here his tears
Would well). 'How could hanybody *do* it to'n?

Look at'n there, upon the cross of glory,
His poor hands and feet, the dear of'm, the *dear* of'm . . .'
He made it sound not like an old story,
But like a real son — his own son.

Well, he is dead, I suppose, though I never heard,
And, I suppose, his native carn his cairn.
I hope they sent him off with his own tune, Blaenwaern.

Perry

Perry thought every country had a moon.
One moon per island. She was insular.
Over a brother's letter I saw her frown:
'Have they got the same moon in America?"

When Uncle John died, Perry shunned company,
Kept to the two-roomed house where she was born.
Stubbornly accomplished her suttee
Sitting for years at her cornish range, alone.

All sounds profaned her, church- or icecream bells.
Were it anything outside her, even grief,
It would have been a shocking waste of life.
But it was Perry's self, and nothing else.

Ready for a tart chat if anyone called,
Even pleased, I think; but readily inclined
To readmit the silence that appalled
Us with the weight of what we left behind:

Her hands folded, guarding the pearshaped growth
She would not have cut out; prodding the flame.
Stranger, holier, than art. So set to take
Possession of her death before it came.

The Match

He spent an hour on the old recreation ground
Kicking conversions from all angles,
Then, the light fading, explained to me the technique.

Did you know my father? I said.
Of course, he replied. I thought of him
Running, close to full-time, along the touch

Trilby-hatted trying to will the Reds
To score a try in the corner. *I haven't been
To a match for fifteen years*, I said. Old trench-

Face said, *Is it the violence, the kicking and
Gouging? No* I said *it's the death*, tears spurting
From my sleeping eyes, *it's the death, the death.*

Amy

Whispered to us, so he shouldn't overhear,
'It's Harold's cousin Bertie. He's deaf-and-dumb.'
Crying through laughter, laughing through tears,
Tears a reflection of happiness held within,
As Bertie held music, or as a creek
People liked coming to and birds sang around.

Stamps

Albums of laughing brethren on the *Berengaria*
Shoulder to shoulder slanting against the wind,
A bride or two among them, shielded like candleflames.

Family registers in great Bibles
Cherishing the still-born
As the pleiades their lost sister.

And the next of the same sex
Given the same name, living two lives.
The dead stamps still terribly thumps. Telegrams

From my Uncle Willie,
Stuck first in Tolima, then in Muswell Hill
With a nervous bloom: 'Holiday postponed. Belle ill.'

Auntie Cecie scuttling with the bad news
Flapping, from house to house. The sky dark
As the sunk granite terrace and beginning to drizzle.

The dead are simply in Santa Monica.
Remembering their birthdays,
The old aunts put stamps before food.

The Mixer

Freddie mixed cement, mixed metaphor
And reality. My father engaged by the boss
With recollections of the perils of typhus
In India — how you had to make sure,
When children went out with the nanny for the day,
All their water was boiled — Freddie took note,
Hunched over, and rose scornfully when he had gone.
'What a bleddy man, i'n it, 'Arold, what a bleddy man!
Sendin' his children out with a bleddy goat!'
Yet overhearing a nurse, stooped by a bed,
Say, 'You're very low,' Freddie came flying
Down the ladder, his cherubic round face grey:
'Bleddy nurse, just told a bleddy man he's dyin'.'

Is Freddie right, who was always wrong before?
Is Harold, dust-lagged, richer than Franz Hals'
Cavalier, throwing back his head
In laughter falling like cool dew on all
Who build whatever houses house the dead?

Stud

He's harvester among the carn rocks. Wives
Let him trump them after the village-drives.
What plums the moist flour when the widows bake?
Colours the shy maids, fruity as saffron cake?

Lighting up, he focuses the dry wit
Outside the chapel. Who looked ripe for it.
They rib him on the stains found in his car.
The evenings draw in. Winter's his threshing-floor.

A boyish chuckle in the grizzled stubble.
He had, when you were leaving home, or troubled,
A silence-covering way of saying 'Yes',
Several times over, with a gruff rising stress,

That consoled; and is loved like the brambled wheals,
Or the contours of snow clinging to some fields,
Farms, slopes, engine-houses and stacks,
Longer than others, when the east wind's backed

Atlantic-wards: each time the same shapes
Of determined white on the dark tilted landscape.
Autumn, he buys back what he's given: the chapel
Mellow with the firstfruits, wheat and apple,

The blessing crackling into auction, women
Ablaze with hats of violet, pink, lemon,
The preacher-auctioneer wrenching his stud
Off, in the spirit, his jolly face a blood-

Orange, Will offers wine-gums round the basses,
Grins wickedly down at the sea of faces,
Nods here and there, and bids first for the gross
Marrow, to shrieks in God's sweet granite house.

Sunday Evening

Eddie hovering, searching for one last loud
Chord, closing his eyes in bliss,
Hearing it fade in my father's soulful ending.
Leslie unveiling his score, a touch of class,

A refining fire, to his wife's ivory smile
Like a mild orgasm. Finger to lowered brow,
Retired Eddie's expressionless wink

At whoever caught his expression.
Cecie scuttling out to make the tea.
Nellie's 'Wonderful music', with a request
For 'Wanting You'. Eddie re-installed. Soaring
My mother as my father plunged. And plunged
As his carrot-haired cousin like a seraph soared
In 'Watchman what of the Night?':

Virginal middle-aged Owen, whose wild eyes
Conveyed the same amazement, whether he prayed
His beloved to come to his arms, in 'Nirvana',
'As the river flows to the ocean',
Or laughed at his own jokes without a sound.
Ethel deaf. None of them, thank God,
For Nirvana this time around.

The Honeymoon Voyage

We have felt lost before,
I tell your mother as the dead
Ship's engines nose through the silent
Mist, and her infirmity
Weakens as home slips further out of reach,
Carn Brea nor Basset Carn, two hills
Of ice slice past us, a monstrous floe

Drifting from Labrador.
The bunk that is our marriage-bed
Pitches through still more violence.
I kiss her tears, confetti
Thrown in a graveyard, her dark eyes beseech
Gentleness I give, our two wills
Melt again into one drifting flow,

And her eyes shine like ore
In the airless cabin. Her head
Lies on my shoulder. In her sigh, love
Leans back to you and pities
Your agony, but we lie each to each,
Wintered yet like your daffodils
Shooting early in the Cornish snow

Moist wind driving ashore
Is beginning to melt. Ahead,
I tell your mother's childlike
Vision, is Yosemite
Again, and the blue rollers of Long Beach,
The small home on Beverly Hills
I built for her, our first car you know

From photographs. Death's more
Beautiful, I tell her, than red-
woods, Sonora's wild lilac,
With a generosity

Warmer than Santa Clara's vale of peach-
trees and apricot, flanked by hills
The golden lemon verbenas grow

So lush on, Livermore . . .
Santa Monica and Merced,
San Francisco's Angel Island,
That creek, Los Alamitos,
Palm Springs . . . Didn't the sight of them outreach
My promise? Remember Soulsbyville's
Strange trees . . . our drive to Sacramento?

Trust me, I tell her, for
The last time I returned I led
You, little more than a child when
We parted, to a city
So wonderful it took away your speech . . .
And she trusts me, while her grief spills
Naturally with the honeymoon snow.

3

Voyage

Lych-gate upon her eyes, death cup her in hands
as tenderly as she would hold a sparrow,
pass here, the rich choices of a poor child,
pass here, the delicacy of a young girl,
sickness and health, her first sweet love bite:
who scolded me, who chose to ignore it,
a black-haired beauty then a white-haired beauty,
in her lap the whole ground, immovable,
my mother, here, my mother, here,
one solo dominates, I hear from habit,
one voice reiterates her tenaciously
like the lead stove she poked up, winter dawns.
Place she placed my father, waits to deflower
her, smooth away the knots of old age
and ways, fact of her death, pass here, way
to myself, gold ring to ring, voyagers
to America again, her seasick eases. Light,
four old men can bear, from boyhood knew them.

Day

We've mouths in plenty, and amazing
rumours of our severe seniors
can't keep pace with us, their paper assets.
Your soul's a kid glove, we shan't outwear it,
come, smile, kid it, brief is our light,
nocturne's perpetual I'll order my end but
day I'm betting on, day, we've centuries
dying, millions die this second, your scent is
dying, why, we alter, but millions are dying, senses
die in a day, come, millions have melted, your
mouth's a turbulence now, O I'll miss
out greater abysses, in wider, push it,
not often the sky this high will blush your room.

(after Catullus V)

Flesh

Let me ache, indicate, simper who touched
your warm cunt, whisper, let on now,
disperse them into our love.
Who did you? it's all the same:
deep pricks or, islands of assiduous fictions,
disperse them into our love.

Am I in her, pummel her, he fucked you, ah
total and thousands of indecent, poked it in
did he, turgid and slewed, my girl, you right
there immixed with another, convoke it actually
wrapt round him, feel his engorgement
displacing your space, cleaving your achable
cleft better than this, novel then sweetly
a habit, why that's my spirit,
my fluttering clairvoyant, my fat ghost.

Sirmio

Pain, almost, an island's, almost-an-island's pain,
whether we turn in the same direction to sleep,
sleeping together drifting to together-
asleep, her arm loosely round me,
or whether nightly having loved and argued together
I take the onus of leaving, repugnant, peregrin,
a day older going down the same flights: where it's
blackest, the stars soon reform, a field of labourers,
salvagers, a million ovens baking in each one
gold as her window still on, unlidded eye, a lake, I
leaving, trees gusting, a torn nail could catch her room.

Pain

Blood thicker than water . . . daughter . . . son.
Lidless exposure. The black sun.
Both your wives . . . your son . . . your daughter.
All night the ice words. Torture of water.

Damien's dismemberment. The tight lips.
Four horses of his apocalypse.
Affable agent. Shirt for the nude.
Strokes. You weep in gratitude.

Jesus, dawn is beautiful.
You stumble home in one piece still.
But there's no safety in the light.
Healing leeches bleed you white.

Rachel is jealous, Leah kind.
And who will lie at your right hand,
at your right hand when you are dust?
You cannot answer, yet you must.

Venice

Like fiery glass we've twisted you
into our own fantastic shapes.
The corsets of your courtesans were nothing
to the bonds we've strapped you in. We've poured

you into paint and, the world's oldest ghetto,
made your windows face inwards on yourself.
I've heard your nightmares much too close for comfort,
and stretched a shaking hand for cigarettes.

Or can you, Venice, as I conceive this dissolute
and subtle lady, feed our dreams and create them
by being bound in your luridly chaste belt?
So that your lord himself, returning,

finds that your whole soul has reknit? Will you drown us?
Or shall we wake one day to find you are
the single tear on the cheek of the Torcello
virgin, that tall slim lady carrying God?

Weddings

Girls

Churning it in up tight you wean us: come serve it us can't
sing in rhythm, O take us, extend it, we're fir-cones ignited,
stick hurt us, wide in, out, permit it here, exhilarate,
noon tomorrow exile you weary, we can't look at our parents.

I means us, henceforward, I means us!

Youths

Penetrate quite all, we're men now and in labour,
nose and eye o mingled, alive who can divide us or release?
Those with worried minds, salt them, commit them to boxes.
Stickier, jam, you sip, a hint, respond it, hairy, lick a bit.

I means us, henceforward, I means us!

Girls

Yes but quick we'll offer to, it's crude but, our rings on,
so why not, our mothers' complexions must have caught fire
too, our reticent mothers, the birth-cleft levels us,
eat, you wean us, go further, we're casting up ashore.

I means us, henceforward, I means us!

Youths

Yes but look hello your cunts are a bush-fire,
we're not yet old enough to beat down the flames,
where's the white pepper stars you blew in your parents' eyes?
We're not sure pray us where we should tool it, harder,
wide ought we or dive us feel we sick or rotate us, whores?

Girls

Yes spear us no peace can equal it tool it you name

.   .   .   .

Youths

Our one idea now's a sleepy reversion.
What love is we know not but that its question
you've quickened us to ask,
now quiet our minds require no answer.

.   .   .   .

Girls

What flowers inside us in secret
                                is plighted to hurt us,
convulse us all through, notice already our breast-bites.
Ride then, come tenderly, deflower us again we're hungry,
seek the virgins that stay in us intact, carry them away,
cover us as you promised with flowers of pollution,
graze in us, you can't have meant it, but careful, pool all this.

       I means us, henceforward, I means us!

Youths

Gentle though, prone on us, summon us, yes but slowly,
ankles now up to our hips, no lie we're trees, see you win.
Drink too the pungent jugs, tails, on our lips, virgins,
nothing's repugnant to equal it, why your fathers did tipsy
their lips with your mothers, those quibblers paired closest,
all their virginity's toasted, your parents are adepts,
third part of their lives was threshing, the pattering seeds,

Girls

and we're now the sun's toast: lip your hairy dew on us
quick penetrate our ass milk drummed out and simultaneous.

       I means us, henceforward, I means us!

(after Catullus LXII)

4

Portraits
(to the memory of Akhmatova)

Nothing visits the silence,
   No apparition of lilac,
      But an inexplicable lightness
         I sense when I breathe your name.
It's not All Souls'. The planet
   Spins on without you, Anna.
      You're now the Modigliani
         Abstract. No candles flame
To amass shadows. Light elected
   You. Annenkov's portrait . . . erect head
      That tilts with a swan's curve
Towards the Neva, towards the living
   Surge of the iced river
      That will not stop nor swerve
But plunge, if need be, within you . . .
   Till room and time started spinning,
      I've gazed, I've tried to splinter
         With love that smiles at stone
This photo of nineteen-twenty,
   The only one where your tender
      Pure and gamine face, grown
One with the page you've entered,
   Blurs at the lips, half-surrenders
      A smile . . . And your lips open
         To me, or familiar Chopin . . .
      It must have been a dream.
But dreams are something substantial,
   The Blue Bird, the soft embalmer.
      It doesn't smell of catacombs
There, and your black fringe is no nimbus.
   A cathedral bell tolls dimly.
      The unmoving stylus hums.
So deep has been this trance,
   Surely its trace fell once,

Caught your eyes and startled you,
Between the legendary embankment
And your House on the Fontanka?

I, like the woman who
Had touched the healer's soul,
Find everything made whole
In your poetry's white night,
Envy the poor you kept watch
With, outside the prison; the touch
Of a carriage-driver, your slight
Hands bearing down with a spring, one
Moment in the tense of his fingers.
Poems outlive a Ming vase,
But your ageing portraits bring me
The rights of a relative
To grieve. Tonight alone I could spare
All that is written here
To restore the chaos where
The Neva deranges your hair,
You laugh, weep, burn notes, live.

Orpheus in Hell
(in memory O.M.)

Perhaps if he praised Death? . . .
They might spare her.
But what came to him was a flight of starlings.

He had never known such torture.
He dragged in a writing-desk,
He sharpened a pencil, laid out a sheet

Of white paper, and made himself sit.
But before he could find a line about Death
He was up and pacing the close and lightless

Room and his lips were moving
Joyfully, his image of her
As the earth's menstruation

Had started up an image of poppy-fields
Blowing red in the clean wind.
He ground his teeth

And made himself sit down again
At the hideous blank paper
And she tried to help him concentrate

By pretending to be asleep
Since it was impossible for her to walk out
And leave his lips free to compose.

He tried to praise her death,
But he was up and pacing on his worn shoes
With a lyric of how her warm lips couldn't

Hide their wakefulness, and she opened her eyes
And smiled, and, smiling, he groaned,
Sat down at the desk and scrawled something.

And in time his Ode to Death saved her.
They were content to keep him only.
She rose to life with a whole notebook of poems

That had seeped like immortal living gum
Out of the dead wood of his death ode,
And every morning she ran it through

In her memory, and every night,
So that the trees and rocks still moved with it.

Dante in Purgatory

This lying in two places
pretending each alone is true
where in fact both are:

both where the love is
at a still centre
with Beatrice, and where

it's whirled without end on
black winds of our own
making, with Francesca:

is not easy,
when a star glimmers
in Hell, or in Heaven

reflection of unheard
lightning below the horizon . . .
gently to turn away each face.

The Marriage of John Keats and Emily Dickinson
in Paradise

This is no dream, the soul is flying south.
Further in summer than the grass,
And past the fields of gazing grain,
And past the stubble-fields of Ruth,
The cold hill side opens, your breast's a flame.

Shiver, a loaded gun.
The throat's a nightingale too full to sing.
Eternal lids apart,
Your eyes the colour of the sherry
Left by the parting guest.

I died for beauty, you for truth.
Fret not after knowledge, I have none.
Experiment escorts us last.
One Gabriel and one Sun
Protect our armouries;
For love is all there is.

The Substance

What is this substance I call glass
she makes? Invisibility
only one side of which I touch.
When I breathe on it I see,
between myself and all I am,
her name, transparently.

Where we slept the facing wall
is a redoubling of the glass
she makes — invisible
but with a ghost's reflectiveness,
the inside of a crystal ball,
the past and all it meant to us

and means: a painful incompletion
I discover was complete.
Once, the substance came by chance
apart in my hands and gave a fleet
and overwhelmingly recalling
fragrance of her I'll not repeat.

A crack ignorable and sheer
in something I can't get behind
that a wind shakes from roof to floor
catches the noon and makes me blind.
Books allow my hand so near,
needle and thread I cannot find.

A Revelation

He sat on the rock writing.
It was cool there, birch-trees had grown up around it.
It was his confession and justification.
He grew lost in abstract thought he closed his diary.

When he opened it again he found a leaf
Pressed like a bookmark at his son's name.
He knew whose hand had plucked it from the trees.
Forests of coal had gone to its making.
Dulled, it was the greenest leaf in the forest.
He stroked it as he had stroked her wrist.

If he could capture the joy that was shaking him
As the wind rocked the trees!
His hand was so quavery he laughed out loud
Sending the birds startled and flying.
'And I saw a new heaven and a new earth.'

The Young King Prophesies Immortality
(St Ethelbert)

Never shall the bride-sleep fall on me.
This index nail's white bruise, and my arm
Numb from sprawling reading Origen.
'Know that you are another world in miniature,
And in you are the sun, the moon, and also the stars . . .'
Know too that death is a matter of depth
Within the apartment-house of limitless storeys
That stretches around the curved shore
Of a desolate lake. Do you fear eviction? Yet
Were you ever *not* here? You look out over the dark lake
From your own window, shivering at the silence.
But to the flier whose shadow skims the lake,
St Michael or Garuda, all the lights,
On all the floors, are blazing . . .

Elegy for Isabelle le Despenser

(At Tewkesbury Abbey is a lock of red-brown hair, belonging to Isabelle, Countess of Warwick, and dated 1429)

Better than stones and castles were my bones.
Better than spears and battles were my tears.
Better than towers and rafters was my laughter.
Better than light and stained glass was my sight.
Better than grate and boar-spit was my hate.
Better than rush and tapestry was my flush.
Better than gold and silver was my shiver.
Better than gloves and falcons was my love.
Better than hymns and pilgrims were my limbs.
Better than crests and banners were my breasts.
Better than tombs and effigies was my womb.
Better than art and ikons was my hurt.
Better than crypts and candles were my friendships.
Better than leaf and parchment was my grief.
Better than mass and matins was my chatter.
Better than swans and bridges were my yawns.
Better than wool and weaving was my breathing.

Remember Isabelle le Despenser,
Who was as light and vivid as this hair.
We are all one.
She sees the clouds scud by, she breathes your air,
Pities the past and those who settled there.

Vienna. Zürich. Constance.

(In May 1912 Freud visited the town of Constance, near Zürich, to spend a weekend with a sick colleague. Jung was deeply hurt that he had not taken the opportunity to visit him in Zürich; Freud equally so that the younger man had not come to see him in Constance. Their relationship, already strained, ended abruptly soon after.)

It was a profound unmeeting.
The train on the branchline from Zürich to Constance
Held a carriage which held a compartment
With a white seat-cover with an impression of Dr Jung,
Slit eyes, in a pugnacious bullet head,
By no means the merry young man of his old age.

The young woman opposite, bright
In a black-and-white striped dress, a blue neck-scarf,
Did not chat to the man not clutching his brief-case
But read through the short journey, smiling occasionally,
Nor did she follow him out at Constance
Where he was warmly embraced by an older man.

The train on the branchline from Constance to Zürich
Held a carriage which held a compartment
With a white seat-cover with an impression of Dr Freud,
His face graven with battles, genial-eyed.
The young man opposite in a modern, very
Tight brown suit with a heavy Victorian watch-chain

Was not startled by the old gent not leaning forward
And not telling him with a twinkle why he had stammered
Momentarily over the word Constance,
But rubbed his hands dreamily and gazed out.
Nor did he help him with his case at Zürich
Where he was greeted cordially by his son.

By a strange coincidence
The young woman who would have been in Jung's
                                        compartment
Had Jung been travelling, was the mistress
Of the young man who would have been in Freud's
                                        compartment
Had Freud been travelling. Having confused
Their plans, they passed each other, unaware.

Waiting for him in her hotel at Constance,
The young woman stepped out of her rainy clothes.
Her fur hat momentarily became a vulva.
Waiting for her in his hotel at Zürich,
The young man stared irritably out of the window
And saw an uncanny light pass across the sky.

Emma and the children leaving the table,
The sage head darkly reflected in its polish
Did not gracefully accept the modified libido theory.
Gazing into the waters of Lake Constance,
A fatherly hand resting on his shoulder,
Jung did not smilingly abjure his mystical drift.

Freud dined sombrely with the faithful Binswanger,
And pleaded a headache. Jung worked late. Owls hooted.
In their uneasy sleep the two exchanged their dreams.
Snow fell on the Jungfrau. Lenin dreamlessly slept.
The centuries slowly drifted away from each other.
In Emma's kitchen-drawer a knifeblade quietly snapped.

Blanche Pain
(found-poem, from a church newsletter)

Mrs Blanche Pain lost her husband Victor after a long anxious
time.
Victor used to grow the most wonderful flowers
For our harvest services every year.
Mrs Josephine Humm, with her daughter, starts a new life
After many years of painful suffering with her husband
Wilfred,
Thank God he is now freed from pain.
Our Organist John Hooker found James Martin dead in his
bed;
Our sympathy goes to Rosemary, his widow.
No more will he be a holiday preacher; life presents us often

With the unexpected. However, we have other news;
Mr & Mrs Howes had a happy celebration, 25 years wed;
They came to me to be married. Mrs Frank Palmer
I hope will soon be back with us after an anxious time.
So many wonderful things happen amidst the gloom
So I say let's give thanks and listen to the 'Still, Small Voice'.

I have been watching in odd moments our organ builders;
The tiniest little pieces go to make up the musical sounds
That we soon hope to hear. After all, God sent His Son
As a little baby to get us to understand
The meaning and the value of small things.

Good luck to Mr & Mrs Bob Pyle who move to Broadstairs
To start a new life.

The Return

Empty the room behind him, the usual
Bach and books, from chairback to chairback flew
tense cats, as if myself released from hospital
I sat shakily, and it wasn't till my shoe

touched something that I thought I saw her
there next to me in her armchair,
saw her very nearly — peeled, as it were
a stick-insect, her long black hair,

heavy white half-naked breasts, her blue
dressing-gown, from the pink-flowered chair,
and gasped, before I could bite my tongue, *Sue!*
I could have sworn you weren't here!

(opened her eyes, like a child in sleepwear
warm and sleepy from the bath, she shone),
began to take in her being almost there,
just as I had taken her being almost gone.

In Her Imagined Person

Why — all senses roused — is he deaf, is he blind?
— Not that deepest darkness is all black,
Even in Shakespeare's black play, his twenty-fourth;
Nor that the exquisite rack
Never drags out the truth
In which she lies, madonna playing whore,

Through her betraying, all too faithful voice;
Though limbs may work like thieves
With time against them
To dynamite a door;
Though desire is a magician's sleeves
Where what he wills, he finds, —

For eyes adjust to midnight,
Even without stars and moonlight,
Even without window-frames,
Enough to tell the particular star
That has fallen, leaving its ice-world, and melted
Into your arms.

It's just that there's no arguing with
The stubborn girl, eternity.
Shy as snowfall, trembling
Like a full cup not to be dashed aside,
And with more rents than a tree,
She will come rustling, keen-eyed, to her choice

Unworthy of this rape, and naked slide
Her breath to his so close it is his own,
And he surrenders all to her surrender,
The unrecognised, the known,
Heartless, and tender,
The stranger and the bride.

Stone

The first book of a poet should be called *Stone*
Or *Evening,* expressing in a single word
The modesty of being part of the earth,
The goodness of evening and stone, beyond the poet.

The second book should have a name blushing
With a great generality, such as *My Sister Life,*
Shocking in its pride, even more in its modesty:
Exasperated, warm, teasing, observant, tender.

Later books should withdraw into a mysterious
Privacy such as we all make for ourselves:
The White Stag or *Plantain.* Or include the name
Of the place at which his book falls open.

There is also the seventh book, perhaps, the seventh,
And called *The Seventh Book* because it is not published,
The one that a child thinks he could have written,
Made of the firmest stone and clearest leaves,

That a people keep alive by, keep alive.

Lorca

Lorca
walking
in a red-light
district at night
heard one of his own songs
being sung
by a whore

he was moved
as if the stars
and the lanterns
changed places

neither the song
to himself
belonged
nor the girl
to her humiliation
nothing
belonged to anyone

when she stopped singing
it went on

death must be a poor thing
a poor thing